I0644074

PLAYING

Around the World

Joanna Brundle

LIGHTBOX
openlightbox.com

LIGHTBOX

Go to
www.openlightbox.com
and enter this book's
unique code.

ACCESS CODE

LBXW5229

Lightbox is an all-inclusive digital solution for the teaching and learning of curriculum topics in an original, groundbreaking way. Lightbox is based on National Curriculum Standards.

OPTIMIZED FOR
- ✓ **TABLETS**
- ✓ **WHITEBOARDS**
- ✓ **COMPUTERS**
- ✓ **AND MUCH MORE!**

Copyright © 2020 Smartbook Media Inc. All rights reserved.

STANDARD FEATURES OF LIGHTBOX

AUDIO High-quality narration using text-to-speech system

VIDEOS Embedded high-definition video clips

ACTIVITIES Printable PDFs that can be emailed and graded

WEBLINKS Curated links to external, child-safe resources

SLIDESHOWS Pictorial overviews of key concepts

INTERACTIVE MAPS Interactive maps and aerial satellite imagery

QUIZZES Ten multiple choice questions that are automatically graded and emailed for teacher assessment

KEY WORDS Matching key concepts to their definitions

VIDEOS

WEBLINKS

SLIDESHOWS

QUIZZES

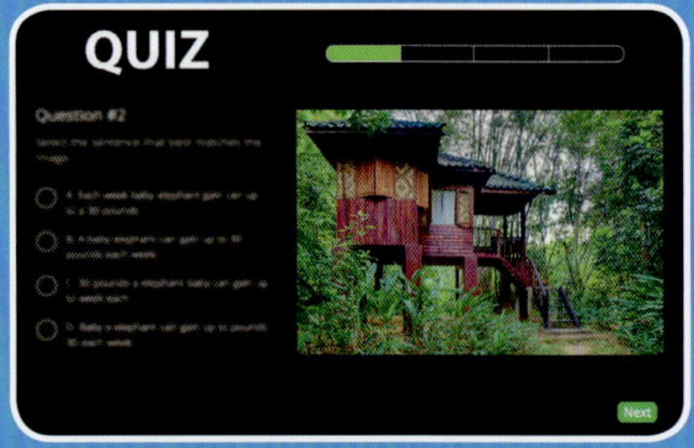

PLAYING

Around the World

Contents

On the Map

In this book, you will read about games from different countries. To see where these countries are, turn to the map on page 22. The countries where these games are played are highlighted there.

Team Players

Children all over the world enjoy playing sports. They enjoy being part of a team and playing to win.

In the **Philippines**, children sometimes get together to play basketball.

Approximately **45 million** children in the United States play on a sports team.

Ice hockey is popular in **Russia**. Players try to hit the puck into the other team's goal. They wear helmets, pads, and gloves to protect them.

These children in **Thailand** are playing polo. It is like hockey on horseback.

Outdoor Games

Playing outdoors is a great way to get some fresh air.

Hopscotch is thought to have started in **China**. It is still played there today.

When it snows in **Sweden**, children have snowball fights. They sometimes build snow walls to hide behind.

Like many children, kids in **Vietnam** enjoy playing a game of "Follow the Leader."

In autumn, children in **England** often go outside to play in the leaves that fall on the ground.

Indoor Games

All children enjoy playing board and card games.

Monopoly is the most played board game in the world. It is sold in more than 114 countries, including **Germany**.

Most countries have their own version of Ludo, but the goal is always to get all your pieces home before anyone else. In **France**, Ludo is called "Little Horses."

Ten pin bowling has been played since the 1800s. It is now popular all over the world. It is especially popular in the **United States**. You can play at a bowling alley like this one.

You can even play at home!

Imagine This!

All around the world, children love using their imaginations to play.

This little boy in **Spain** is pretending to be a cowboy.

This boy in **Ghana** might be acting like a lion or tiger.

This little boy in **Guinea-Bissau** is having fun playing in this box. A box can be a fort, a boat, a car, and much more.

This girl in **Australia** might become an animal doctor when she gets older.

Water Play

Children everywhere love to swim and splash.

People in **Thailand** celebrate New Year's Day with a special water festival, called Songkran. Children enjoy splashing and using their water guns.

In **Guinea**, splashing around in a river is a fun way to spend an afternoon.

Norway has plenty of places for children to play on the beach.

Street children in **Nepal** can sometimes be seen cooling off in the fountain.

Swing, Skip, and Run

Playing can be a way to get active. It can be fun to move around.

This child in **Indonesia** enjoys swinging on a piece of cloth.

Children ages 5 to 17 should have at least **60 minutes** of exercise every day.

"Tag" is a running game played all over the world. In **China**, it is called "Catch the Dragon's Tail." The children form a line. The leader is the dragon's head. He or she has to catch the dragon's tail at the other end.

These children in **Botswana** are using a piece of rope for their skipping game.

Wheel Play

Children around the world love to have toys with wheels. Sometimes, the wheel is the toy!

This little girl in **Mongolia** is taking a ride in an electric toy car.

These boys in **Vietnam** are having just as much fun in their home-made wooden cars.

This boy in **Burundi** is playing with a toy truck made out of old wire.

In **Benin**, old tires are great to roll around the neighborhood.

Party Time

Playing games is a great way to celebrate a birthday.

Children in **England** love to play "Pass the Parcel" at parties. Every time the music stops, someone gets to unwrap part of the gift.

"Pin the Tail on the Donkey" is a popular party game around the world. In **Japan**, it is called Fukuwarai. Children are blindfolded and have to stick eyes, noses, mouths, and ears onto cutout faces.

Children in **Mexico** often have a piñata at their parties. Guests are blindfolded, and then take turns to hit the piñata with a stick. When it breaks, candy and other treats fall to the ground for everyone to enjoy.

San José Buenavista, Mexico, is known for piñatas. With 1,000 residents, there are more piñatas than people.

Clap and Sing Along

Children everywhere love to play clapping games. They clap to a rhythm and often sing as well. Singing is a part of many games.

In **Brazil**, children sing nursery rhymes they call *cantigas de roda*. In “Ciranda, Cirandinha” they sing and chant while holding hands.

These girls in **India** are playing “Miss Mary Jab Choti Thi.” They clap to the beat and act out parts of the song.

Many countries have traditional singing games. In **France**, a popular song is “Frère Jacques.”

Some singing games also include dancing. In **England**, children dance in a circle when they play “Ring-a-Roses.”

See where the games in this book are played.

1. Australia
2. Benin
3. Botswana
4. Brazil
5. Burundi
6. China
7. England
8. France
9. Germany
10. Ghana
11. Guinea
12. Guinea-Bissau
13. India
14. Indonesia
15. Japan
16. Mexico
17. Mongolia
18. Nepal
19. Norway
20. Philippines
21. Russia
22. Spain
23. Sweden
24. Thailand
25. United States
26. Vietnam

Arctic Ocean
Atlantic Ocean
Pacific Ocean
Indian Ocean
Southern Ocean
ASIA
EUROPE
AFRICA
AUSTRALIA
1
2
3
5
6
7
8
9
10
11
12
13
14
15
17
18
19
20
21
22
23
24
26
Legend
Where Games Are Played
Land
Water
N
1,000 Miles
SCALE
1,000 Kilometers

KEY WORDS

Research has shown that as much as 65 percent of all written material published in English is made up of 300 words. These 300 words cannot be taught using pictures or learned by sounding them out. They must be recognized by sight. This book contains 109 common sight words to help young readers improve their reading fluency and comprehension. This book also teaches young readers several important content words, such as proper nouns. These words are paired with pictures to aid in learning and improve understanding.

Page	Sight Words First Appearance
4	a, all, and, being, children, get, in, of, on, over, part, play, sometimes, the, they, to, together, world
5	are, into, is, it, like, other, them, these, try
6	air, great, have, some, started, still, thought, there, way
7	go, leaves, many, often, that, when
8	always, before, but, home, little, more, most, own, than, their, your
9	at, been, can, even, has, now, one, this, you
10	around, be, boy
11	an, animal, car, girl, might, much, or, she
12	day, people, river, water, with
13	for, off, places
14	every, move, run, should
15	end, he, head, line
16	as, just, made
17	old, out
18	eyes, faces, stops, time
19	take, then, turns
20	along, call, hands, miss, song, well, while
21	also

Page	Content Words First Appearance
4	basketball, Philippines, players, sports, team, United States
5	gloves, goal, helmets, hockey, horseback, pads, polo, puck, Russia, Thailand
6	China, games, hopscotch
7	autumn, England, fights, ground, kids, leader, Sweden, Vietnam, walls
8	France, Germany, goal, horses, Ludo, Monopoly, pieces, version
9	ten pin bowling, bowling alley
10	cowboy, imaginations, Spain
11	Australia, boat, box, doctor, fort, fun, Ghana, Guinea-Bissau, lion, tiger
12	afternoon, festival, Guinea, New Year's Day, Songkran, guns
13	beach, fountain, Nepal, Norway
14	cloth, exercise, Indonesia, minutes
15	Botswana, dragon, rope, tag, tail
16	Mongolia, ride, toys, wheels
17	Benin, Burundi, neighborhood, tires, truck, wire
18	birthday, donkey, ears, Fukuwarai, gift, Japan, mouths, music, noses, parcel
19	candy, guests, Mexico, parties, piñatas, residents, San José Buenavista, stick, treats
20	beat, Brazil, India, nursery rhymes, rhythm, singing
21	circle, dancing

Published by Smartbook Media Inc.
350 5th Avenue, 59th Floor New York, NY 10118
Website: www.openlightbox.com

Copyright ©2020 Smartbook Media Inc.
All rights reserved. No part of this publication may be reproduced, stored in a retrieval system, or transmitted in any form or by any means, electronic, mechanical, photocopying, recording, or otherwise, without the prior written permission of the publisher.

Library of Congress Control Number: 2019939926

ISBN 978-1-5105-4392-8 (hardcover)
ISBN 978-1-5105-4393-5 (multi-user eBook)

Printed in Guangzhou, China
1 2 3 4 5 6 7 8 9 0 23 22 21 20 19

062019
122918

Project Coordinator: Heather Kissock
Art Director: Terry Paulhus

Every reasonable effort has been made to trace ownership and to obtain permission to reprint copyright material. The publisher would be pleased to have any errors or omissions brought to its attention so that they may be corrected in subsequent printings. The publisher acknowledges Alamy, iStock, and Shutterstock as the primary image suppliers for this title.